MW01488744

Rejected

FOUR WEEK MINI BIBLE STUDY

Heather Bixler

Becoming Press, LLC

Heather Bixler/Becoming Press, LLC
www.becomingpress.com

Cover image from Light Stock by Lisa Forseth

Ordering Information:
Quantity sales. Special discounts are available on quantity purchases by corporations, associations, and others. For details, contact the "Special Sales Department" at the website address above.

Rejected - Four Week Mini Bible Study/ Heather Bixler—1st ed.

ISBN-13: 978-0983468523
ISBN-10: 0983468524

Scripture quotations are from The World English Bible.

Table of Contents

Introduction

Rejection in my life started when I was very young. At around 8 years old, I was bullied in school for no other reason than I didn't live in a nice house and I was overweight.

I'm pretty sure this rejection carried with me through my adult life because I still struggle with the feelings of not being good enough. I still look to find my worth in the people who let me into their "groups" and even through those who I feel still reject me. Often I strive to be accepted by certain people thinking that maybe if they accept me, or even acknowledge me, then I will finally be good enough.

As an adult I have experienced rejection in every facet of my life. I have also rejected and hurt others in my life. Even though I believe that we need to have boundaries in all relationships, I also believe that even through those boundaries we can still accept and love the other person and embrace acceptance instead of rejection.

Does this mean we should allow hurtful people in our lives? No, simply because rejection is an action where we go out of our way to tell someone they are not good enough. If someone is going out of their way to make us feel unworthy then that is a good indicator that person does not deserve to have influence over your heart, and how you live your life.

I'm a firm believer that if I'm resisting writing something then I should most definitely write. Topics of rejection and acceptance are not something I would purposefully set out to write about. But as God has revealed to me, I write to the broken because I am broken.

This Bible Study is not coming from a writer who has mastered the desire to be accepted, or overcome her fear of rejection. This study comes from a broken person who has been rejected throughout her life and is seeking God to find healing.

I truly pray that this Bible Study is a blessing to you and you are able to find healing too.

WEEK ONE

Rejection is a Lie

He came to his own, and those who were his own didn't receive him. - **John 1:11**

So many years of believing that what I did made me good enough has held me back from the life God had planned for me. Oh how disappointed I was to find out that even if I tried my best - someone or something - would say, "You're not good enough." It was everywhere and I couldn't get away from it.

In high school I remember thinking I had algebra down, that I understood it, and had no idea why everyone thought it was so hard. But every time I thought I had every single answer right on a test, to my dismay, my teacher would mark a lot of them wrong. It was so discouraging and eventually I just gave up on school because it felt like no matter what I did it was never good enough, even though I thought I was capable of doing the work.

Isn't that how life is sometimes? We try our best only to be discouraged to find out it's not good enough.

> Maybe we're not looking for good enough, maybe instead we are looking for perfection.

So often when we are rejected by life, or other people, we harbor this lie that we are not good enough. Perfection doesn't mean good enough. When we seek acceptance from others we often put on the actions we must take, and the hoops we must jump through, in order to please them. But perfection doesn't mean you are good enough. ***The pursuit of perfection means you are insecure in who you are and what you are capable of doing. Perfection is pride.***

Honestly, rejection is a lie, and we all know who is the father of all lies. If someone rejects you - they are believing a lie. If you reject someone else - then you are believing a lie. If we live a life in our pity and reject God, His blessings, and our gifts then we are believing a lie. If we believe we are not good enough then we are rejecting God and all He has blessed us with, and we have been duped into believing the lie of the enemy.

Rejection is a lie.

The truth is this: God made you in His image, and that makes you capable. Not by what you can do, not by what you have learned, but by His grace. Grace to shower His love on us, grace for creating us in His image and with a free will, and grace to bless us with the gift of the Holy Spirit.

> If we want to be released from the bondage of rejection or not feeling good enough then we need to recognize it as a lie.

We need to stop rejecting our self.

SO often we have been rejected, that we reject our self. We hold back the gifts God has given us. We compare our self to other people. We are ashamed of our mistakes. Guilt says you're not good enough. *When we reject our self we reject God because God is alive in our heart through the power of the Holy Spirit.*

Shortly before I was set to release my eBook "Breaking Pride" I posted on Facebook that my new eBook was going to be released the next day IF I didn't chicken out first and delete it. Someone on my Facebook page encouraged me and said something along the lines that God gave me the gift to write and to not throw it away. It occurred to me that I was struggling with my own pride, and I was struggling with my fear of rejection. In that moment I realized I needed to continue with publishing the eBook because I was tired of rejecting God and the gifts He had given me.

Also, Jesus talks about how it is a sin to bury the gifts God has given us in the parable of the talents in Matthew 25:14-30. In this parable we are reminded that it is best to be a good steward of what we've been given instead of burying it in the ground out of fear and rejection.

Rejection is all about us, it's all about the flesh. Rejection is a lie from the enemy that we have chosen to believe. **Acceptance is all about God. Acceptance is the truth.**

Are we weak? Yes. Are we perfect? No. Do we have all the answers? No. Do we need to have all the answers to live a life accepted? No. God has already accepted us and He will equip us. But in order for us to live a life accepted we must first realize the truth and we must begin to LIVE it out. That truth is we are accepted by God always, and rejection is a lie.

Life Application

> *"If we believe we are not good enough then we are rejecting God and all He has blessed us with"*

Even thought rejection is an action, it is a result of a lie that is being believed. List three situations where you felt rejected. What lie was fueling that rejection?

Week One Scripture Journal

Week One Memory Verse:
Psalm 118:22.

Day One: Write down the scripture you are learning in the space provided below:

Day Two: Write scripture down four times on a sticky note and place them around the house.

Day Three: Look up 3 different versions of the scripture. Write them in the space provided below:

Day Four: Write scripture 10x's in the space provided below:

Day Five: Read Psalm 118 and journal your thoughts in the space provided below:

Day Six: Write scripture by memory 3x's in the space provided below:

Day Seven: Share your scripture with a friend.

Discussion Questions

The following questions are designed to be used within a group discussion about the scripture you memorized.

- Name three promises of God you found in Psalm 118.
- What can you expect to receive once you let go of the lie of rejection? What happened in Psalm 118?
- What should we do when we feel rejected or if we are in times of trouble?

HEATHER BIXLER

What Does Rejection Look Like?

Brothers, even if a man is caught in some fault, you who are spiritual must restore such a one in a spirit of gentleness; looking to yourself so that you also aren't tempted.
- **Galatians 6:1**

Understanding the difference between rejection and establishing boundaries is key when it comes to making sure we aren't living in the lie that is rejection. First, we need to look deeper into what rejection is, we've already talked about how it is a lie, but here is what rejection looks like:

• When we reject someone we refuse to use their skills or abilities.
• When we reject someone we do not consider them.
• When we reject someone we refuse to acknowledge them or give them affection.
• To reject someone is to throw them away.

Rejection is a pretty harsh attitude towards another person. The last one really hits a button with me because that's what it feels like most often when someone rejects me, it feels as if they are throwing me away.

As I journey through this area of my life I really want to make sure that I am not personally rejecting someone in my life. I often ask myself ,when is rejection OK? However I think we might confuse rejection with establishing healthy boundaries and they are two completely different things.

Rejection is when we see someone who is hungry or thirsty and we turn our back on them and act like they are not there. Rejection is when we treat someone with hatred and there is no compassion in our heart towards them. Often rejection is a result of pride. We may reject someone because we think we are better than them, or we may reject someone because we are angry at them.

> The difference between healthy boundaries and rejection is the condition of our heart and why we are placing space between us and the other person.

Even if the relationship is harmful and results in sin, you can still detach yourself from the relationship with a heart that is right and compassionate. Jesus said to forgive and pray for your enemies. If there is a relationship where you are being physically hurt, it's OK to move on from that relationship without having any contact with that person. I don't think anyone would expect someone to stay in a relationship where there was sexual or physical abuse, or where their children are being harmed physically. In fact Jesus said in the Bible that sexual sin is the only exception when it comes to divorce (Matthew 5:32.)

The problem with rejection is that it comes from a heart that is fearful, wounded, and prideful.

Relationships are unique and every one is different; however rejection can be avoided with a shift in our attitude and a change in our heart towards that person.

Acceptance doesn't require entrance into a relationship. Acceptance just requires a heart that is forgiving and compassionate.

When I think of acceptance I think of God sacrificing His only son on the cross in order to accept us. Did He say that sin no longer existed? Did God say we could now do whatever we wanted? Does sin still separate us from God? It does by our own choice. But God has accepted us. With that one sacrifice He showed us that He will always be there for us, in the background waiting, and when we are ready we can be closer to Him.

Sometimes the sin of another person causes the rejection in their life. We may want to love them, and our hearts may accept them, but they may still choose their sin over receiving that love and acceptance. Rejection is a result of believing a lie, and they are giving into the lie that sin will fulfill their life.

Rejection is an attitude that results in an action that looks a lot like putting space between you and someone who has hurt you. How do you know it's OK to step back from certain relationships? It's only rejection if your heart is not aligned with the heart of God.

Life Application

> *"Rejection is an attitude that results in an action that looks a lot like putting space between you and someone who has hurt you."*

Think of a relationship that you have had to disconnect from.

- What are your thoughts about that person?
- Are they thoughts of bitterness, anger, hurt?
- Do you feel you are better than that person?
- If all of these emotions were gone and you were able to find understanding, compassion, and even a little bit of love towards this person hiding somewhere in your heart, would you still want to be disconnected from this person?

We need to examine our heart when it comes to how we feel about another person. Once we know where our heart stands then we will know if we need to disconnect from the relationship or not. We will also know if we are rejecting them, or if we are setting up a healthy boundary.

Week Two Scripture Journal

Week Two Memory Verse:
Romans 15:13

Day One: Write down the scripture you are learning in the space provided below:

Day Two: Write scripture down four times on a sticky note and place them around the house.

Day Three: Look up 3 different versions of the scripture. Write them in the space provided below:

Day Four: Write scripture 10x's in the space provided below:

Day Five: Read Romans Chapter 15 and journal your thoughts in the space provided below:

Day Six: Write scripture by memory 3x's in the space provided below:

Day Seven: Share your scripture with a friend.

Discussion Questions

The following questions are designed to be used within a group discussion about the scripture you memorized.

- What does God desires us to do for those who are weaker in their faith?
- Why does God want us to accept one another?
- Using Romans chapter 15 write down a prayer you can say for the troubled relationships in your life.

HEATHER BIXLER

Acceptance

Come, and hear, all you who fear God. I will declare what he has done for my soul. I cried to him with my mouth. He was extolled with my tongue. If I cherished sin in my heart, the Lord wouldn't have listened. But most certainly, God has listened. He has heard the voice of my prayer. Blessed be God, who has not turned away my prayer, nor his loving kindness from me. **- Psalm 66:16-20**

After a moment of rejection, I sat on my couch praying to God to encourage my heart and He gently replies with *"Will my encouragement really make a difference?"*

He had already been encouraging my heart and I didn't believe it or trust it. I chose to believe the lies more, and He was right, His encouragement didn't really make a difference because I was rejecting His truth. That's when I realized that the defeat I had felt was only there because I chose to keep it there.

Will everyone accept us? No. So how do we live a life accepted instead of living a life based on the lie of rejection – we need to learn to accept our self first.

Our acceptance begins with embracing our flaws and weaknesses. Acceptance always begins with an open hand and a little bit of trust. When we accept a hand shake or a gift we don't know the full story of who the person is, or what may be inside the wrapped present. But we trust that it is something special or the person is trustworthy.

When we learn to accept our self we do so without knowing the full story, and we do so knowing that we are accepted by God, flaws and all. Then we can walk this life with confidence based out of a trust in God and His promises.

> Acceptance gives us the power to reject the lie of rejection. We can finally say this is not who I am and this is not the life God has planned for me.

After I got over my pity party of rejection, I finally got the nerve to get up and continue on with what God DID have planned for me. Even if I failed, I was going to do it. Even if I wasn't very good at it, I was going to continue on down the path because ultimately there is no other path I would rather be on.

Acceptance gives us the power to move forward even if we aren't good enough, even if we fail, because acceptance embraces the whole journey, failures and all.

Life Application

"Acceptance gives us the power to reject the lie of rejection. We can finally say this is not who I am and this is not the life God has planned for me."

• Do you feel that moving forward with something you are not familiar with or have no experience with is foolish?

I would like to challenge your view of foolishness. Read the story of Abraham (Genesis chapters 12-24).

• How many times did He move forward in God's will for His life but He seemed unqualified to do so?
• Was Abraham a fool?
• Define fool with your dictionary.
• Define fool with your own words.

Week Three Scripture Journal

Week Two Memory Verse:
Luke 10:16

Day One: Write down the scripture you are learning in the space provided below:.

Day Two: Write scripture down four times on a sticky note and place them around the house.

Day Three: Look up 3 different versions of the scripture. Write them in the space provided below:

Day Four: Write scripture 10x's in the space provided below:

Day Five: Read Luke Chapter 10 and journal your thoughts in the space provided below:

Day Six: Write scripture by memory 3x's in the space provided below:

Day Seven: Share your scripture with a friend.

Discussion Questions

The following questions are designed to be used within a group discussion about the scripture you memorized.

- How can our fear of rejection stop us from doing God's will in our life?
- Why do you think Jesus tells His disciples not to take a purse, bag, or sandals with them and not to greet anyone on the road?
- What idols are holding you back from walking fully in God's will for your life?

Will God Reject Me?

Yahweh, don't rebuke me in your wrath, neither chasten me in your hot displeasure. For your arrows have pierced me, your hand presses hard on me. There is no soundness in my flesh because of your indignation, neither is there any health in my bones because of my sin. For my iniquities have gone over my head. As a heavy burden, they are too heavy for me. My wounds are loathsome and corrupt, because of my foolishness. I am pained and bowed down greatly. I go mourning all day long. **- Psalm 38:1-6**

Every day I wake up with this fear that if I make a mistake God will reject me even though I know in my heart that He will never leave me or forsake me.

It took me awhile to realize the difference between making a mistake and totally rejecting God and His commandments. It is truly my desire in life to delight in Him, and further His kingdom. My heart wants to reject the lies, and my idols. Truly I want to live in my Faith rather than use it to get what I want or to satisfy my flesh.

Often we are brought up in church where scripture isn't clear, or God's motives aren't clear. We think God is angry at us, or is waiting to just use us. Or maybe we are on the other side of the spectrum and find that God

41

loves us so that must mean we do not need to change our lifestyle – maybe then we can have our cake an eat it to, often I hear, *"God just wants us to be happy."*

Honestly the Bible doesn't talk about "being happy" or being a puppet of the Lord. Does God have a purpose for us? Yes. Does He desire for us to follow and choose Him? Yes. Does God reject us if we don't? No.

> The truth is if we are feeling rejected by God then it is because we have rejected Him.

I often think of the story in the Old Testament about the Israelites (see Numbers chapter 21) and how they rejected God and God allowed fiery serpents to enter to where they were in the wilderness. He allowed the serpents to enter because the Israelites rejected Him and did not want to serve Him, but rather serve their idols. But once the fiery serpents came the only One they had to turn to that could do anything to help them was God. Don't you know God gave them a way out, even though they rejected Him? **He was still there waiting to help them, all they needed to do was ask.**

God is always there waiting with His arms stretched out. I know it doesn't seem like it at times, but every time the Bible talks about God rejecting His people it is because they rejected Him. Rejection by God does not mean He will leave you. We can reject Him and still find Him when we call on Him. His gift of grace is always there, we just need to accept it.

> When we reject God we are rejecting His grace.

To me that shows God's humility. Even God knows rejection, and even God knows regret.

One of God's promises is that He will never leave us nor forsake us. God is not in the business of rejection. Jesus paid the price for our eternal acceptance into heaven, and into God's presence through the Holy Spirit..

God is willing to use our mistakes to help teach us. Often, when we are afraid to make a mistake it is because we are afraid of losing one of our beloved idols, whether it be money, our good reputation, our life, or our friends. Unfortunately, we are willing to reject God in order to keep the thing we fear losing

> In those moments it's easy to think God isn't listening and God isn't giving us any answers. Until we let go of the thing we are afraid of losing we really aren't turning to God for the answers because we are still trying to control the outcome.

If we are going to love and accept God we are going to have to learn to take risks, walk in Faith, and seek His truth in everything, whether we like the answer or not. We need to let go of our idols. When we let go of those idols we will hear God's voice loud and clear, and we will know the direction we need to walk in, and will have the faith to walk in that direction instead living in the fear that always seems to hold us back.

Life Application

> *"The truth is if we are feeling rejected by God then it is because we have rejected Him."*

- What decisions do you feel confused about right now?
- Why are you confused about these decisions?
- What is the fear behind your confusion?

Sometimes we look for the big YES from God, but if we are looking for the YES we may be confused because our heart might be rejecting that YES out of fear or control. Sometimes we need to pray for the big NO concerning a decision. God is willing to clearly show you where a path is the WRONG path. But sometimes our heart isn't really open to the path that is the RIGHT path, so we assume God isn't giving us any answers. If God isn't saying NO and you are still confused, it is time to examine what fears and idols are truly holding you back from taking the path that He is leading you to.

Week Four Scripture Journal

Week Two Memory Verse:
John 3:17

Day One: Write down the scripture you are learning in the space provided below:

Day Two: Write scripture down four times on a sticky note and place them around the house.

Day Three: Look up 3 different versions of the scripture. Write them in the space provided below:

Day Four: Write scripture 10x's in the space provided below:

HEATHER BIXLER

Day Five: Read John Chapter 3 and journal your thoughts in the space provided below:

Day Six: Write scripture by memory 3x's in the space provided below:

Day Seven: Share your scripture with a friend.

Discussion Questions

The following questions are designed to be used within a group discussion about the scripture you memorized.

- Why are we condemned if we do not believe in Jesus?
- What do people love more than light?
- Why are we already condemned?

HEATHER BIXLER

The Breakthrough

So how do we overcome rejection in our life? Let's face it not everyone is going to respect you and accept you for who you are. But there comes a time when we need to learn how to move past this rejection so we can move forward in the call God has on our life.

For me it took a day when I was tired of letting what other people thought of me be more important than anything else. Acceptance by other people can become an idol in your life like it did mine.

One day I looked at my kids and I repented to God because I realized what other people thought of me was more important than enjoying their presence and being their mom. It was so important that I was unable to see God's amazing blessing sitting right in front of me.

I looked at my husband and I repented to God for being mean, bitter, and angry towards him because of the hurt others had caused in my life.

I looked at God and I repented the fact that I cherished other people's opinions of me more than I did the blessing He had given me, and the encouragement He speaks to my heart on a regular basis.

Then I had to forgive. I forgave others for rejecting me and the gifts God has given me. I forgave myself for rejecting people as well and for hurting others the way I was hurting.

It's not easy feeling unwanted. When we place the desire to be accepted as an idol in our life we feel unwanted because we are unaware of God and His love and sacrifice for us. We see the lie that we are not good enough and believe we are unwanted instead of embracing the truth that we are worthy of God's love and already accepted by Him.

> God wants us, but in our idolatry of yearning to be accepted by other people, we do not want Him.

We are rejecting God, the gifts He gave us, and amazing blessings around us.

We need to get to a point in our life where we are tired of rejecting those closest to us just so we can be loved by everyone else.

> That's our breakthrough; realizing our idol and releasing that idol through repentance and forgiveness.

Then we can pour out our heart. No one wants to pour out bitterness and anger in their life, but when we desire acceptance by other people more than God, that's exactly what's in our heart!

When we release this idol we are finally free to pour out a heart filled with the Holy Spirit and love of God. We find our compassion and our understanding. Our joy has been opened up and is no longer hidden beneath the lies.

We can finally pour our heart out for Christ. Our words can flow out with truth and grace. There is no more fear to be who God created us to be. No more worrying about what other people will think, because we choose to seek what God thinks and follow His direction no matter what.

There is freedom in releasing this idol. It will take some work, and you will need to face the pain that comes with breaking every idol and every chain. But through repentance and forgiveness, that pain will go away and be replaced with Joy.

About the Author

Heather is a mom of three, married to a firefighter, and she is a writer. She is passionate about sharing God's word in a practical and loving way.

He has said to me, "My grace is sufficient for you, for my power is made perfect in weakness." Most gladly therefore I will rather glory in my weaknesses, that the power of Christ may rest on me.- **2 Cor 12:9**

Follow Heather

- **Author Blog:** HeatherBixler.com
- **Twitter:** @hbixler03
- **Facebook:** HeatherBixlerWrites
- **Pinterest:** @hbixler03
- **Instagram:** @hbixler03

Audiobooks

If you like audiobooks then be sure to check out Heather's audiobooks on audible and iTunes!

Reviews Needed!

I would love to hear your feedback - please leave your reviews of *Rejected - Four Week Mini Bible Study* online wherever books are sold!

More Resources

To view more practical Bible Studies visit:

http://becomingpress.com

More Books by Heather

Be You – Four Week Mini Bible Study

Breaking Pride: Tearing Down Walls, Walking in His Grace

Desires of My Heart: Meditation on Psalm 37:4

Devotions for Moms: Thirty-Seven Devotionals

Faith – Four Week Mini Bible Study

Hope – Four Week Mini Bible Study

Love - Four Week Mini Bible Study

My Scripture Journal: Fearing the Lord

My Scripture Journal: Gratitude

My Scripture Journal: The Promises of God

My Treasures - Four Week Mini Bible Study

Rejected - Four Week Mini Bible Study

Worship is This - Four Week Mini Bible Study

Made in the USA
Middletown, DE
16 December 2019

Rejected

FOUR WEEK MINI BIBLE STUDY

In this four week mini Bible Study you will discover the power of acceptance in your life; the acceptance we all have from God, and why it's important to accept our self, flaws and all.

Rejection is a powerful force in our life and our Christian walk. It effects our confidence in God and His call on our life, but little do we know the power we have to let go of the control it has on us.

Rejection is also an attitude that results in an action that looks a lot like putting space between you and someone who has hurt you. In this Bible study you will learn how to overcome the power or rejection over your life.

WWW.BECOMINGPRESS.COM

ABOUT THE AUTHOR

heather bixler

Real Life, real faith, real answers. Heather is passionate about sharing God's Word in a loving and practical way. She also loves coffee, blogging, and making her house a home for her family. Heather is a motivator who loves helping her family and friends "reach for the stars" and see the dreams and goals God has placed on their hearts become a reality. You will find truth, inspiration, and real life in all of her writing.

ISBN 9780983468523

90000

9 780983 468523